The Seneca

People, Culture, and History

by Dr. Faye Lone

CAPSTONE PRESS
a capstone imprint

Published by Capstone Press, an imprint of Capstone
1710 Roe Crest Drive, North Mankato, Minnesota 56003
capstonepub.com

Library of Congress Cataloging-in-Publication Data is available on the Library of Congress website.

ISBN: 9798875208669 (hardcover)
ISBN: 9798875208614 (paperback)
ISBN: 9798875208621 (ebook PDF)

Summary: The traditions, culture, and history of the Seneca people are told through engaging text, sidebars, activities, maps, and more.

Editorial Credits
Editor: Erika L. Shores; Designer: Heidi Thompson; Media Researcher: Rebekah Hubstenberger; Production Specialist: Tori Abraham

Image Credits
Alamy: Alex Hamer, 10, Stock Montage, Inc., 20, Zachary Frank, 24; Associated Press: Don Heupel, 12, 19; Bridgeman Images: © Pitt Rivers Museum, 16; Getty Images: Carlos Osorio/Toronto Star, 6, iStock/ Kristine Radkovska, 25 (bottom), MPI, 15, PHOTOSTOCK-ISRAEL/SCIENCE PHOTO LIBRARY, 14, Yu Chun Christopher Wong/Eurasia Sport Images, 7; Hayden Haynes, cover, 28; Metropolitan Museum of Art: Ralph T. Coe Collection, Gift of Ralph T. Coe Foundation for the Arts, 2011, 18; Peace Queen (Jigönsahse), watercolor by Ernest Smith (Tonawanda Seneca, Heron Clan), 1936. Courtesy of the RMSC, Rochester, NY., 9, The Trappers, watercolor by Ernest Smith (Tonawanda, Seneca, Heron Clan), 1940. Courtesy of the RMSC, Rochester, NY., 13; Photo Courtesy Peter Jones, 26; Samantha Jacobs, 27; Shutterstock: 23, Bardocz Peter, 4, MaraZe, 25 (recipe background), Nynke van Holten, 23, Runrun2 (brush stroke), back cover, spine, 1, Zack Frank, 22

Printed and bound in the USA. 006307

TABLE OF CONTENTS

Words in **bold** are in the glossary.

ABOUT THE SENECA

The Seneca Nation is the largest of the six nations that make up the Haudenosaunee (hoe-dee-no-SHOW-nee). The Iroquois Confederacy, or Six Nations, is another name for this group who lived in what is now southeastern Canada and the northeastern United States. Hundreds of years ago, the Mohawk, Oneida, Onondaga, and Cayuga nations joined with the Seneca. In 1722, the Tuscarora Nation joined as the sixth nation.

The Haudenosaunee were an influential group during the first 300 years of European arrival to North America. Haudenosaunee leaders often spoke more than one of their own six languages as well as a European language, such as English or French.

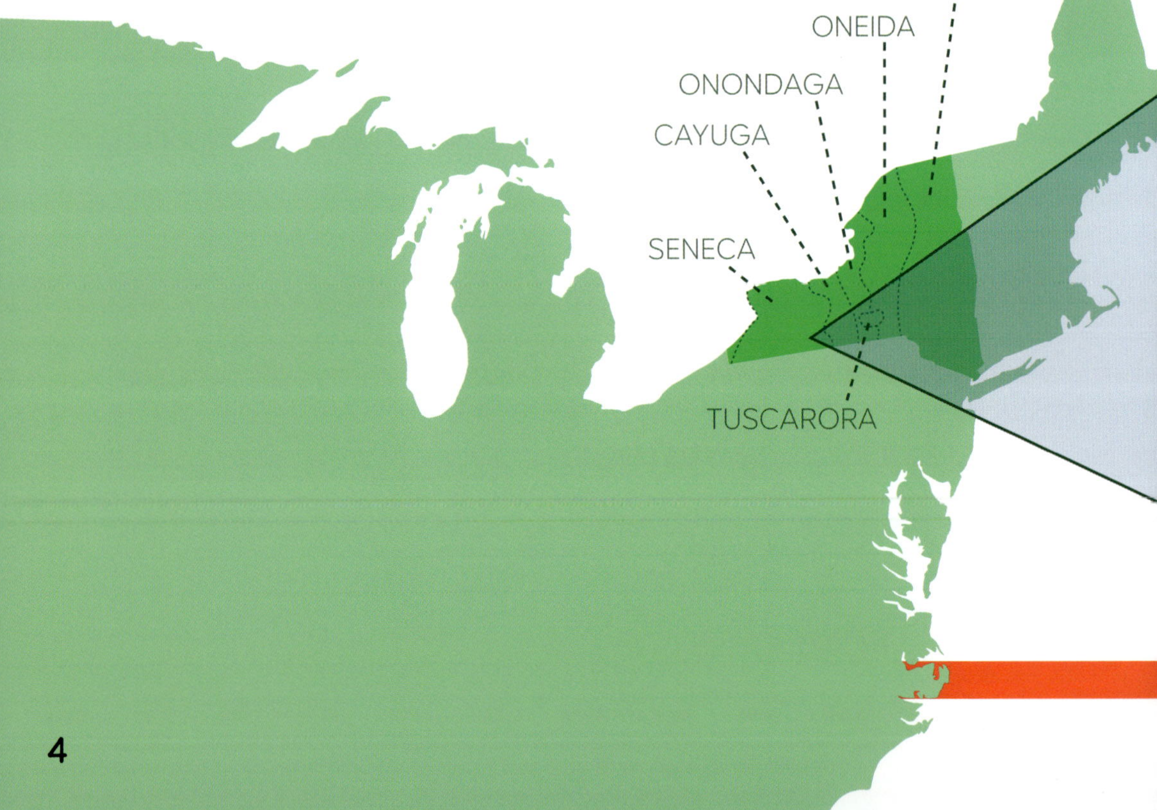

The Seneca Today

Today, the Seneca live in western New York on the Cattaraugus, Allegany, and Tonawanda **reservations**. In addition, Oil Springs in New York is part of Seneca lands. Seneca people also live on the Seneca-Cayuga Reservation in Oklahoma and on the Six Nations of the Grand River Territory in Ontario, Canada.

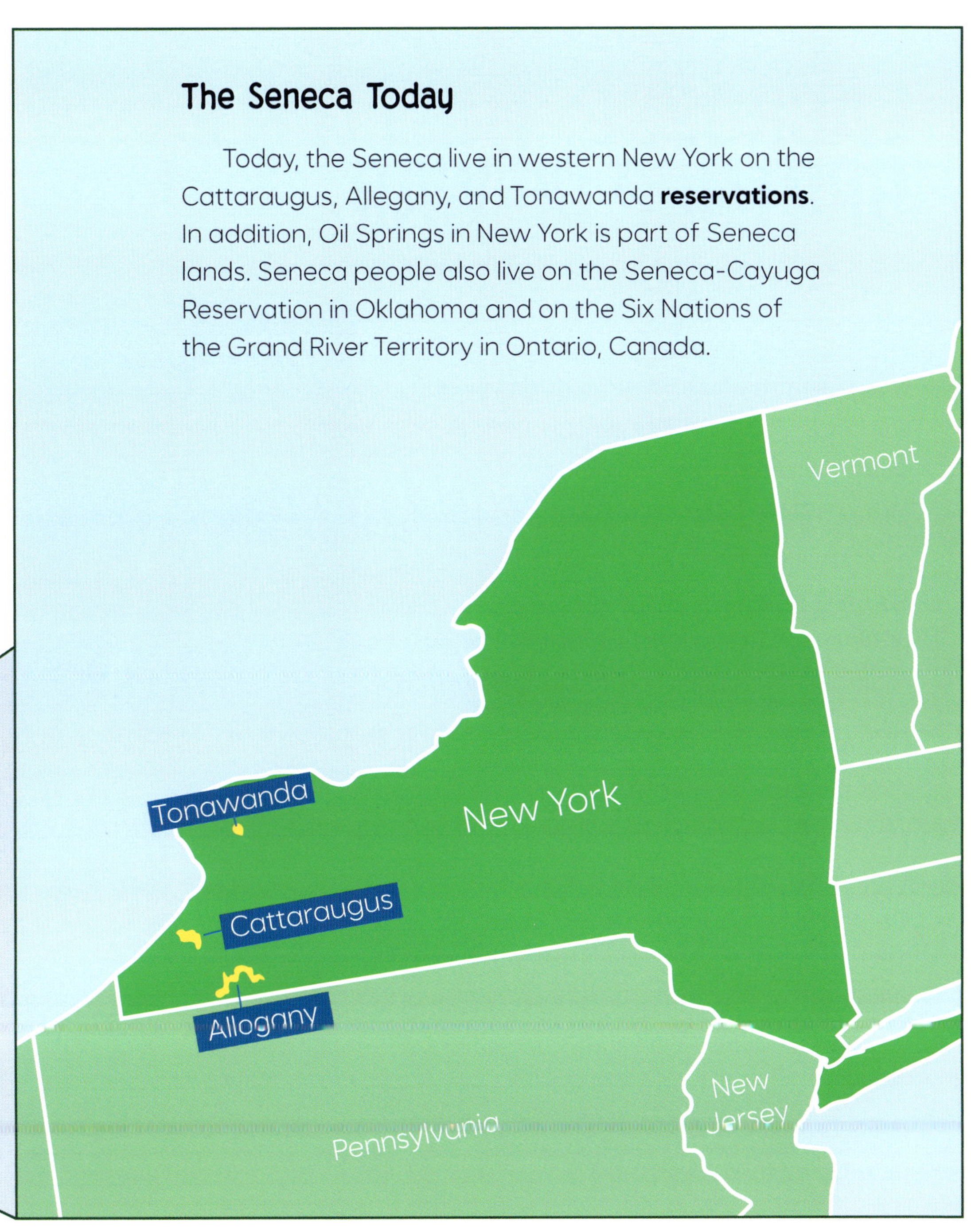

LACROSSE: THE LITTLE BROTHER OF WAR

First known as stickball, lacrosse has been played for 900 years. It is an important part of Seneca **culture.** In the beginning, only men competed. The game was violent. It was even called the Little Brother of War. The game was played with wooden sticks, usually made from hickory wood. Players had to carry the ball to the other team's goal in the "pocket" of the stick, passing the ball between teammates. The game could last days and involve 100 to 1,000 players.

A traditional lacrosse stick

Today, Haudenosaunee children might get their first lacrosse stick when they are very young, sometimes even before they can walk. By the time they finish high school, top players are chosen to play for professional teams or the Haudenosaunee Nationals team that competes against other countries. In 2024, the Haudenosaunee Nationals Men's team and the Haudenosaunee Women's team each won a bronze medal in the World Games. Lacrosse is just one part of Seneca culture that reminds people of their long history and instills pride in their future as a nation.

A Haudenosaunee player competes in the 2024 World Lacrosse Women's championship.

A NATION'S HISTORY

Before joining together, the Haudenosaunee fought each other for a long time. More than 400 years ago, a man called the Peacemaker and Hiawentha (Hiawatha) from the Onondaga Nation spoke to each nation. With the help of Jikonsaseh, a woman from the Onondaga Nation, a peace **treaty** was formed among the Seneca, Mohawk, Oneida, Onondaga, and Cayuga nations. The nations' leaders buried weapons under a white pine tree in the Onondaga territory. The tree is known as the Tree of Peace.

Because the Haudenosaunee controlled the trade routes through northeast North America, agreements or treaties were made with different nations. Since there was no written language, **wampum** belts were made to symbolize the agreements between two groups. People had to memorize the words so they could be repeated and remembered over the years.

Jikonsaseh (far left) helped bring about peace among the nations of the Haudenosaunee.

The wampum belts still exist. The nations' people still learn what they mean. Wampum is made by making tube beads out of two different seashells, the whelk and the quahog. It takes a long time to make just one bead, so the belts take a very long time to finish.

The Hiawatha Belt marks the agreement among the nations of the Haudenosaunee. The squares represent each nation, with the tree symbol representing the Tree of Peace at Onondaga. The belt was made long before European **colonizers** arrived. The original belt is kept by the Onondaga Nation.

Two Row Wampum

A second important belt is the Two Row Wampum, made in 1613. This belt has two rows of purple beads, same size, not touching each other. It tells of the agreement with the Dutch and the Six Nations that the groups would be equals. Separate nations; equal, like brothers. And they agreed not to interfere with the other's business. To "stay in your own canoe." This type of agreement was made with other nations as well.

Design a Wampum Belt

Wampum belts were the way the Seneca and the rest of the Haudenosaunee made agreements with other groups. An agreement is where you make a promise to do something with someone else.

What You Need

- graph paper
- pencil

What You Do

Using graph paper, fill in the "beads" to make a wampum belt to represent an agreement. You could make an agreement with a teacher to do your homework. Or maybe you make an agreement with a caregiver to clean your room. Or you make an agreement with a friend to be friends forever.

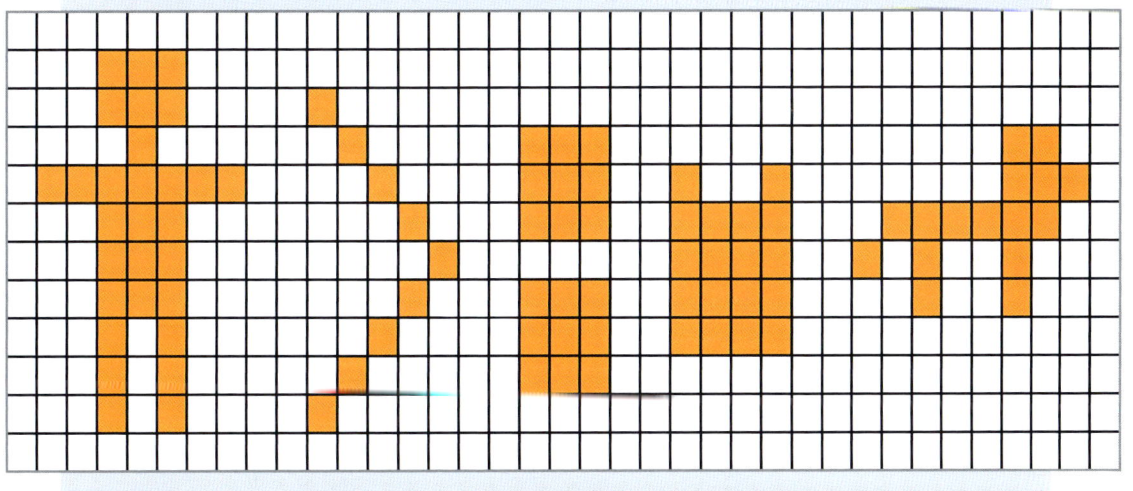

Person **Going Forward** **Books** **Bed** **Dog**

You can make up any shape to create your belt. Then tell the story about what you are making an agreement to do. Share with others.

The Seneca traded with the Europeans who came to their territory. A common trading item was metal. The Seneca used wooden bowls, clay pots, and flint stone for everyday items. When iron, copper, and silver were brought by Europeans, they traded for Seneca items such as animal hides. Beaver hides were a favorite of Europeans. The fur made fancy hats and other items that the rich people of Europe liked to wear. With the metals, the Seneca would now have large iron pots to cook in. Jewelry was made from pewter, iron, or brass at first. Later, silver came into use in the 1700s. Brooches were used as pins for decorations and were highly prized. They are still made and worn today.

The Seneca made and used clay pots for cooking.

The Seneca hunted beavers, raccoons, and other animals and traded their fur for metals from Europeans.

Cloth trade was important between the Seneca and Europeans as well. There is even a treaty where Senecas are supposed to get calico cloth as part of the agreement. That treaty is still upheld by the state of New York and the Seneca today. But the cloth given now is a cheaper, plain cloth. This agreement allowed traditional Seneca clothing to be made from cloth instead of deer hides. The dresses became fancier to look more like the European style of the 1800s.

The American colonies joined together in 1776 to become the United States. The Seneca, and the rest of the Haudenosaunee, were an example for the **democracy** the colonists created. Each nation had representatives. Each **clan** within each nation had both a male and a female leader. Their power was equal. The colonies created states that would have representatives in two houses of government, the Senate and the House. Unlike the Haudenosaunee, women were not given voting rights under the new U.S. government until 1920.

Red Jacket was a Seneca chief who helped create treaties between his nation and the new United States.

Ely Parker

Ely Parker was a Tonawanda Seneca. He spoke both Seneca and English. He studied law but could not become a lawyer because he was Seneca and not a U.S. citizen. He was an engineer, U.S. Army officer, and an aide to General Ulysses Grant during the Civil War (1861–1865). He wrote the final draft of the Confederate surrender terms at Appomattox. When Grant became U.S. president, he made Parker the commissioner of Indian Affairs, in charge of the government's relations with Native Americans. Parker died in 1895.

In 1779, American forces attacked Seneca and Cayuga towns. Crops, orchards, and stored foods were destroyed. This was to stop Natives from attacking colonial villages and army supplies. The American attacks brought an end to the alliance that the Seneca and other Native people had with the British. This change made the Americans more powerful than the Haudenosaunee. Many more changes were coming.

Haudenosaunee chiefs with the nations' wampum belts in 1871

The Seneca people became separated due to forcible removal by the new United States. Whole villages were made to move to Oklahoma in 1831. Some of the Seneca and Cayuga still have territory in Oklahoma. Some of the Oneidas went to Wisconsin. Some Seneca went as far as Kansas and came back. They had to buy their own land back and that is now the Tonawanda Seneca territory east of Buffalo, New York.

In 1924, the U.S. Congress made a law stating all Native people in the United States would become U.S. citizens. This had two major impacts on the rights of Native nations to govern their own citizens. All Natives would be subject to U.S. federal laws, and Native men could be drafted into U.S. military service. Even without the draft, Native men volunteered for military service. Many of them became highly decorated service members.

In 1934, Congress passed the Indian Reorganization Act. The act changed Native nations' governments from their traditional ways to adopting constitutions similar to the U.S. government. This change further impacted the nations' connections to their traditional ways of life.

Timeline

1570–1600 Haudenosaunee Confederacy forms.

1722 The Tuscarora Nation join the Haudenosaunee as the sixth nation.

1775–1783 The Seneca side with the British during the American Revolutionary War.

1779 General George Washington orders the destruction of Seneca villages.

1797 Senecas lose much of their territory in western New York in the Treaty of Big Tree. The treaty creates reservation land for the Seneca.

1830 U.S. President Andrew Jackson signs the Indian Removal Act. The goal of this act is to move tribes living east of the Mississippi River to Indian Territory in the west.

1831 The Seneca have to leave their lands in Ohio and move to Indian Territory.

1838 The Seneca in New York sign the Treaty of Buffalo Creek with the U.S. government. The Seneca agree to give up their remaining land in New York for land in Kansas.

1842 The Seneca sign the Treaty of Buffalo Creek of 1842, which gives them back their New York reservation land in Cattaraugus and Allegany.

1848 Cattaraugus, Oil Springs, and Allegany Senecas establish an elective form of government. Tonawanda Senecas remain a traditional government and hold the titles (chiefs) for the new Seneca Nation of Indians.

1924 The U.S. government makes Native Americans U.S. citizens.

1934 The Indian Reorganization Act

1987 Seneca village Ganondagan is dedicated as a historic site in New York. A traditional longhouse is built there in 1998.

2015 The Seneca Art and Culture Center opens at Ganondagan State Historic Site.

SENECA CULTURE

The Seneca, and all the Haudenosaunee, are **matriarchal**. That means women play a major part in leadership and making decisions. Traditionally, women controlled the home, farming, food storage, and family matters. Women would even decide if the men were to go to war or not.

There are eight clans of the Seneca. Clans are extended family groups. A person's clan is determined by the clan their mother belongs to. The Hawk, Snipe, and Heron are called Bird Clans. The Beaver, Bear, Deer, Turtle, and Wolf are called the Animal Clans.

Traditionally, jobs and duties were assigned based on clan. During certain ceremonies, clans are divided by Bird and Animal. When someone marries, they are supposed to marry someone from the "other side of the fire," so Bird Clans often marry Animal Clans. The couple then becomes part of the woman's clan.

A Seneca doll made between 1870 and 1880 is a mother carrying a child on her back.

The Bird and Animal Clans that make up the Seneca Nation are shown on the nation's flag.

Traditionally, each clan would discuss the issues of the day among themselves. The clan chief and the clan mother would hear the decisions that the clan would make. Then the chief would go to the tribal council with the chiefs from the other clans. When needed, the chiefs from the Seneca would go to the grand council to discuss matters with the other five nations. Then the decision of the Six Nations would be taken to foreign governments or companies. This kind of government is a true democracy, with everyone having a voice and ways to ensure good leadership.

Today, some of the Six Nations still have their traditional government. Some changed to elective governments when the Indian Reorganization Act was carried out across the United States. The elected leaders serve two to four years. Chiefs are chiefs for life unless they are convicted of a crime.

Seneca clans lived together in villages spread throughout what is now western New York.

The Seneca Language

The Seneca people work to preserve their language. Seneca language classes are held both for children and adults. Recordings of Seneca **Elders** speaking the language help protect the language from disappearing. Here are some words in Seneca to practice.

akso:d (ahk-sode)—my grandmother

ësgö:gë'ae' (eh-sgoh-geh-ay)—I will see you later.

hakso:d (hahk-sode)—my grandfather

ha'nih (hah-nee)—my father

no'yëh (noh-eh)—my mother

nyaweh skannoh (nyah-way skeh-no)—I am thankful you are well.

THE LONGHOUSE BELIEF

Long ago, the Seneca lived in longhouses. These long wooden buildings had a door on either end. Several families lived in one longhouse. In Seneca culture, the longhouse also stands for the importance of community. Longhouse ways teach social responsibility in daily life. By coming together for ceremonies, the people cook together, eat together, sing, and dance. Young boys sit in the middle to learn the songs. Girls are given leadership duties and taught the speeches.

All ceremonies are giving thanks for the different elements of the seasons. Seneca give thanks to the Thunder Beings, to the Maple, to Seeds, to the Strawberry, and so on. All of these things are part of what the Creator has given the people. There's a belief not to ask for things because the Creator has already given everything people need.

People can visit a recreated longhouse at Ganondagan in New York.

An Origin Story

Every culture has an origin story. The story tells how people came to live on Earth. The Seneca, and all the Haudenosaunee nations, share the story of Sky Woman. It is a very long story when told with all the details. This is a shorter retelling.

There was a time when people lived in the sky. One woman, who was pregnant, was living there and was hungry for special fruits from a special tree. One day, the tree fell down, and a big hole was made when the roots were pulled up. The woman went to look down the hole and fell into it. Down, down she fell.

There were birds flying near and some geese got together to catch her and take her safely to a turtle's back. He was swimming in the big ocean when he saw the geese carrying her.

Now Sky Woman could see that she needed more than a turtle's back to live on. So, animals that could swim took turns diving very deep to bring her some dirt from the bottom of the waters. One of the animals was able to bring her some dirt. She used her powers from the Sky World to make the dirt get bigger and bigger to make land for her to live on. The land became very big and is called Turtle Island.

SHARING

It has always been a “shared pot” lifestyle within the Seneca culture. Since longhouses often had many families living inside, everyone was expected to contribute to the entire household. Hunters would bring back game meat, such as deer, duck, and fish. Gatherers would bring back plants to eat. Inside the longhouse, a pot of food in the center was for anyone who was hungry to dip into and eat at any time.

Even today, Seneca share what they have. A mother might take a bag of kid’s clothes to someone they know who has a child who can use them. Hunters bring meat to an Elder’s house or to a big family. When there is a fire or death in a family, the community comes to help.

Inside the longhouse at Ganondagan, people can see the shared cooking pot.

A Seneca Recipe

In Seneca, the name for strawberry means "star flower." People say the strawberry came from Sky World, where the stars are. The wild strawberry is a special medicine plant for the Seneca. Wild strawberries are flavorful. They are very small. Strawberries sold in grocery stores are not grown in the wild and are bigger than wild berries.

Strawberry Drink

Ingredients

- 1 quart strawberries, washed
- 1 cup sugar
- 1 gallon water

Instructions

1. Slice up the strawberries. Then mash them well.
2. Stir the sugar into the mashed berries.
3. Add the berry mixture to the water.
4. Pour over ice.
5. Share this drink with everyone!

POTTERY AND BEADWORK

Seneca pottery was made long before Europeans arrived. Before trade with Europeans brought iron pots, Seneca people made pots from clay. The pots were used to store food, collect water, and cook in. Today, Seneca pottery is still made, but are now considered to be art pieces.

Peter B. Jones

Peter B. Jones is a potter and sculptor. He makes many of his pots in the traditional style of early Haudenosaunee pottery using pit firing and stoneware clay. He studied at the Institute of American Indian Art in New Mexico. His pottery is displayed by community members, art collectors, and museums. Jones has a pottery studio and workshop where he teaches classes for schools and other community groups in the Cattaraugus territory.

Raised beadwork was developed in the 1700s. Seneca artists made items for tourists. Wealthy people rode trains from big cities to the Niagara Falls region to buy souvenirs. Items were made to look like familiar items: birds, shoes, pillows, and picture frames.

Today, Mary Jacobs and Sam Jacobs are award-winning Seneca beadworkers. Sam learned from her mother, which is how this art form has been passed down over hundreds of years. Today's beadworkers use their skills to make art representing Seneca culture. Beadwork items show things important to Senecas, like strawberries, beans, corn, and squash. Known as the Three Sisters, beans, corn, and squash are very important foods. Seneca dried them and then saved them to eat throughout the winter.

Sam Jacobs' raised beadwork is displayed on a picture frame.

DANCING

Powwows are Indigenous gatherings held all over the United States and Canada. They are either traditional, non-competitive gatherings, or competitions. Seneca participate in these gatherings along with people from other nations. There are many styles of powwow dances, for both male and female dancers of all ages. Beautiful **regalia** are made for each type of dance. One set of beadwork can take a whole year. Sometimes, the colors and designs tell which nation a dancer belongs to.

Socials are gatherings in Seneca communities. People eat, sing, and dance together. The Seneca have different dances and regalia than powwow dances. Outfits can be the traditional clothes worn for Seneca ceremonies but are not required to dance.

One Seneca dance is called the Smoke Dance. It began as the War Dance for men. The steps might look like he is hunting. The dancer looks on the ground for tracks or points an imaginary arrow to shoot. Today, the dance has gotten faster. Women can dance to the songs, but their dance steps are not like hunting. The women may move like they are gathering food or cooking. All ages can dance, from toddlers just walking to a person who is 100 years old. Everyone comes together to remember and celebrate being Seneca.

Traditional Seneca regalia features beautiful beadwork.

Glossary

clan (KLAN)—a large group of families and related people

colonizer (KAH-luh-nye-zur)—a nation or government that claims a territory other than its own

culture (KUHL-chur)—the traditions, beliefs, and behaviors that a group of people share

democracy (di-MAH-kruh-see)—a form of government in which people vote for their leaders

Elder (EL-dur)—an older person

matriarchal (may-TREE-ar-kuhl)—having a female as the head of a family or society

regalia (re-GALE-ee-uh)—special clothes that are worn for powwows or other special occasions

reservation (rez-er-VAY-shuhn)—an area of land that has been set aside for a tribe or tribes under an agreement with the U.S. government

treaty (TREE-tee)—a written agreement between two groups

wampum (WAHM-puhm)—beads made from polished shells strung together or woven to make belts

Read More

Bruegl, Heather. *Haudenosaunee*. Ann Arbor, MI: Cherry Lake Publishing, 2025.

Spruce, Darelyn. *I'm a Little Smoke Dancer*. Morrisville, NC: Lulu Press Inc., 2024.

Treuer, Anton. *Everything You Wanted to Know About Indians But Were Afraid to Ask*. Hoboken, NJ: Levine Querido, 2021.

Internet Sites

Seneca Nation of Indians: About the Seneca Nation
sni.org/about

Seneca Iroquois National Museum: Onöhsagwë:de'Cultural Center
senecamuseum.org

Haudenosaunee Confederacy: Historical Life as a Haudenosaunee
haudenosauneeconfederacy.com/historical-life-as-a-haudenosaunee

Index

About the Author

Dr. Faye Lone is an enrolled Tonawanda Seneca, Hawk Clan. She has given cultural presentations to schools and organizations for more than 40 years. She was the Program Director of the Native American Resource Center at Rochester Public Schools in New York. She worked at the U.S. Department of Education in the Office of Indian Education. She obtained a Doctorate of Education from the University at Buffalo. She is also an award-winning artist and uses her art to teach about her Haudenosaunee culture and issues facing Indigenous peoples today.